D1607950

# OF SOULS,

# SYMBOLS, AND

# SACRAMENTS

# JEFFREY R.

# HOLLAND

This book is not a product of the Council of the First Presidency or Quorum of the Twelve Apostles and is not a doctrinal declaration by or for The Church of Jesus Christ of Latter-day Saints. I alone am responsible for the publication of this work, and I alone am accountable for any errors and limitations it may contain.

This material was originally presented in an address at Brigham Young University, 12 January 1988.

**Library of Congress Cataloging-in-Publication Data**

Holland, Jeffrey R., 1940–
  Of souls, symbols, and sacraments / Jeffrey R. Holland.
    p.  cm.
  ISBN 1-57345-859-7
  1. Sex—Religious aspects—Christianity.  2. Marriage—Religious aspects—Christianity.  3. Family—Religious life.  I. Title
BX8643.S49 H65 2001
241'.66—dc21                                          00-065642

Printed in the United States of America       72082-6314

10   9   8   7   6   5   4   3   2   1

*Dedicated*

*to all who*

*want love to last*

# CONTENTS

The topic of human intimacy is as sacred as any I know. In discussing it, the subject can quickly slide from the sacred into the merely sensational. It would be better not to address the topic at all than to damage it with casualness or carelessness.

Some may feel this is a topic we hear discussed too frequently, but given the world in which we live, we may not be hearing it enough. All of the prophets, past and present, have spoken on it. Most in the Church are doing wonderfully well in the matter of personal purity, but some are not doing so well, and much of the world around us is not doing well at all.

Unfortunately, the degree of unchaste behavior around us is likely to increase rather than decrease as the times become more secular, more sophisticated, and more self-indulgent. Edward Gibbon, the distinguished British historian of the eighteenth century, wrote, "Although the progress of civilisation has undoubtedly contributed to assuage the fiercer passions of human nature, it seems to have been less favourable to the virtue of chastity. . . . The refinements of life [seem to] corrupt, [even as] they polish, the [relationship] of the sexes."[1]

But it is not our purpose here to document social problems or wring our hands over the dangers that such outside influences may hold for us. As serious as such contemporary realities are, I wish to discuss this topic in quite a different way, discuss it specifically for Latter-day Saints. So I conspicuously set aside statistics on such tragedies as AIDS, abortions, and illegitimate births and refer rather to a gospel-based view of personal purity.

Indeed, I wish to do something even a bit more difficult than listing the dos and don'ts of personal purity. I wish to examine, to the best of my ability, *why* we should be clean, *why* moral discipline is such a significant matter in God's eyes. I know that may sound presumptuous, but a philosopher once said, "Tell me sufficiently *why* a thing should be done, and I will move heaven and earth to do it." Hoping you will feel the same way as he, and with full recognition of my limitations, I wish to try to give at least a partial answer to "Why be morally clean?" I will need first to pose briefly what I see as the doctrinal seriousness of the matter before then offering at least three reasons for such seriousness.

# THE SIGNIFICANCE OF SANCTITY

Why is the matter of sexual relationships so severe that fire is almost always the metaphor, with passion pictured vividly in flames?

May I begin with one-half of a nine-line poem by Robert Frost. (The other half is worth a sermon also, but it will have to wait for another day.) Here are the first four lines of Frost's "Fire and Ice":

> Some say the world will end in fire,
> Some say in ice.
> From what I've tasted of desire
> I hold with those who favor fire.[2]

A second, less poetic but more specific opinion is offered by the writer of Proverbs: "Can a man take fire in his bosom, and his clothes not be burned? Can one go upon hot coals, and his feet not be burned? . . . But whoso committeth adultery with a woman lacketh understanding: he that doeth it destroyeth his own soul. A wound and dishonour shall he get; and his reproach shall not be wiped away."[3]

In getting at the doctrinal seriousness of this subject, why is the matter of sexual relationships so severe that fire is almost always the metaphor, with passion pictured vividly in flames? What is there in the potentially hurtful heat of this that leaves one's soul—or perhaps the whole world, according to Frost—destroyed, if that flame is left unchecked and those passions unrestrained? What is there in all of this that prompts Alma to warn his son Corianton that sexual transgression is "an abomination in the sight of the Lord; yea, most abominable above *all* sins save it be the shedding of innocent blood or denying the Holy Ghost"?[4]

Setting aside sins against the Holy Ghost as a special category unto themselves, it is LDS doctrine that sexual transgression is second only to murder in the Lord's list of life's most serious sins. By assigning such rank to a physical appetite so conspicuously evident in all of us, what is God trying to tell us about its place in His plan for all men and women in mortality? I submit to you He is doing precisely that— commenting about the very plan of life itself. Clearly God's greatest concerns regarding mortality are how one gets into this world and how one gets out of it. These two most important issues in our very personal and carefully supervised progress are the two issues that He as our Creator, Father, and Guide wishes most to reserve to Himself. These are the two matters that He has repeatedly told us He wants us never to take illegally, illicitly, unfaithfully, without sanction.

As for the *taking* of life, we are generally quite responsible. Most people, it seems to me, readily sense the sanctity of life and as a rule do not run up to friends, put a loaded revolver to their heads, and cavalierly pull the trigger. Furthermore, when there is a click of the hammer rather than an explosion of lead, and a possible tragedy seems to have been averted, no one in such a circumstance would be so stupid as to sigh, "Oh, good. I didn't go all the way."

No, "all the way" or not, the insanity of such action with fatal powder and steel is obvious on the face of it. Such a person running about with an arsenal of loaded handguns or military weaponry firing at young people would be apprehended, prosecuted, and institutionalized if in fact such a lunatic would not himself have been killed in all the pandemonium. After such a moment of horror, we would undoubtedly sit in our homes or classrooms with terror on our minds for many months to come, wondering how such a thing could possibly happen— especially to members of the Church.

Fortunately, in the case of how life is taken, I think we seem to be quite responsible. The seriousness of that does not often have to be spelled out, and not many sermons need to be devoted to it. But in the significance and sanctity of *giving* life, some of us are not so responsible, and in the larger world swirling around us we find near-criminal irresponsibility. What would in the case of *taking* life bring absolute horror and demand grim justice, in the case of *giving* life brings dirty jokes, four-letter language, and wholesale voyeurism in movies, on television, over the internet, and almost everywhere else we turn.

Is all of this so wrong? That question has always been asked, usually by the guilty. "Such is the way of an adulterous woman; she eateth, and wipeth her mouth, and saith, I have done no wickedness."[5] No murder here. Well, maybe not. But sexual transgression? "He that doeth it destroyeth his own soul."[6] Sounds near-fatal to me.

It is this doctrinal seriousness that should help us prevent such painful moments and avoid what Alma called the "inexpressible horror" of standing in the presence of God unworthily. Care and caution in this matter will permit the intimacy it is your right, privilege, and delight to enjoy in marriage to be untainted by such crushing remorse and guilt. May I now give those three reasons I mentioned earlier as to why this is an issue of such magnitude and consequence.

# THE DOCTRINE
# OF THE SOUL

W*hen one toys with the God-given . . . body of another, he or she toys with the very soul of that individual, toys with the central purpose and product of life.*

F irst, we simply must understand the revealed, restored Latter-day Saint doctrine of the soul, and the high and inextricable part the body plays in that doctrine.

One of the "plain and precious" truths restored to this dispensation is that "the spirit *and* the body are the soul of man,"[7] and that when the spirit and body are separated, men and women "cannot receive a fulness of joy."[8] Certainly that suggests something of the reason why obtaining a body is so fundamentally important to the plan of salvation in the first place, why sin of any kind is such a serious matter (namely, because its automatic consequence is death, the separation of the spirit from the body and the separation of the spirit and the body from God), and why the resurrection of the body is so central to the great abiding and eternal triumph of Christ's atonement. We do not have to be a herd of demonically possessed swine charging down Gadarene slopes toward the sea[9] to understand that a body is *the* great prize of mortal life, and that even a pig's will do for those frenzied premortal spirits that rebelled and to this day remain dispossessed in their first, unembodied estate.

May I quote a 1913 sermon by Elder James E. Talmage on this doctrinal point:

"We have been taught . . . to look upon these bodies of ours as gifts from God. We Latter-day Saints do not regard the body as something to be condemned, something to be abhorred. . . . We regard [the body] as the sign of our royal birthright. . . . We recognize the fact that those who kept not their first estate . . . were denied that inestimable blessing. . . . We believe that these bodies . . . may be made, in very truth, the temple of the Holy Ghost. . . .

"It is peculiar to the theology of the Latter-day Saints that we regard the body as an essential part of the soul. Read your dictionaries, the lexicons, and encyclopedias, and you will find that nowhere, outside of the Church of Jesus Christ, is the solemn and eternal truth taught that the soul of man is the body and the spirit combined."[10]

So partly in answer to *why* such seriousness, we answer that when one toys with the God-given— and satanically coveted—body of another, he or she toys with the very soul of that individual, toys with the central purpose and product of life, "the very key" to life, as Elder Boyd K. Packer once called it.[11] In trivializing the soul of another (please include the word *body* there) we trivialize the atonement, which saved that soul and guaranteed its continued existence. And when one toys with the Son of Righteousness, the Day Star Himself, one toys with white heat and a flame hotter and holier than the noonday sun. You cannot do so and not be burned. You cannot with impunity "crucify . . . the Son of God afresh."[12] Exploitation of the body (please include the word *soul* there) is, in the last analysis, an exploitation of Him who is the Light and the Life of the world. Perhaps here Paul's warning to the Corinthians takes on newer, higher meaning:

"Now the body is not for fornication, but for the Lord; and the Lord for the body. . . . Know ye not that your bodies are the members of Christ? shall I then take the members of Christ, and make them the members of an harlot? God forbid. . . . Flee fornication. . . . He that committeth fornication sinneth against his own body. What? know ye not that your body is the temple of the Holy Ghost which is in you, which ye have of God, and *ye are not your own?* For ye are bought with a price: therefore glorify God *in your body, and in your spirit,* which are God's."[13]

Our soul is what is at stake here—our spirit *and* our body. Paul understood that doctrine of the soul every bit as well as Elder James E. Talmage did, because it is gospel truth. The purchase price for our fullness of joy—body and spirit eternally united—is the pure and innocent blood of the Savior of the world. We cannot then say in ignorance or defiance, "Well, it's my life" or worse yet, "It's my body." It is *not* your life *or* your body. "Ye are not your own," Paul said. "Ye are bought with a price." As a result of the excruciating suffering endured by Him in the atonement—the payment *He* made for *our* sins—we are eternally indebted to Jesus. That is one reason we call Him "Master," in the holiest sense of the word. So in answer to the question, "Why does God care so much about sexual transgression?" it is partly because of the precious gift offered by and through His Only Begotten Son to redeem the souls—bodies *and* spirits—we too often share and abuse in such cheap and tawdry ways. Christ restored the very seeds of eternal lives,[14] and we desecrate them at our peril. The first key reason for personal purity? Our very souls are involved and at stake.

# A SYMBOL OF
# TOTAL UNITY

You may come to that moment of real love, of total union, only to discover to your horror that what you should have saved has been spent.

Second, *human intimacy, that sacred, physical union ordained of God for a married couple, deals with a symbol that demands special sanctity.*

Such an act of love between a man and a woman is—or certainly was ordained to be—a symbol of total union: union of their hearts, their hopes, their lives, their love, their family, their future, their everything. It is a symbol that we try to suggest in the temple with a word like *seal.* The Prophet Joseph Smith once said we perhaps could render such a sacred bond as *welding*—that those united in matrimony and eternal families are *welded* together, inseparable if you will, to withstand the temptations of the adversary and the afflictions of mortality.[15]

But such a total, virtually unbreakable union, such an unyielding commitment between a man and a woman, can come only with the proximity and permanence afforded in a marriage covenant, with the union of all that they possess—their very hearts and minds, all their days and all their dreams. They work together, they cry together, they enjoy Brahms and Beethoven and breakfast together, they sacrifice and save and live together for all the abundance that such a totally intimate life provides such a couple. And the external symbol of that union, the physical manifestation of what is a far deeper spiritual and metaphysical bonding, is the physical blending that is part of—indeed, a most beautiful and gratifying expression of—that larger, more complete union of eternal purpose and promise.

As delicate as it is to mention, I nevertheless trust the reader's maturity to understand that physiologically we are created as men and women to form such a union. In this ultimate physical expression of one man and one woman, they are as nearly and as literally one as two separate physical bodies can ever be. It is in that act of ultimate physical intimacy that we most nearly fulfill the commandment of the Lord given to Adam and Eve, living symbols for all married couples, when He invited them to cleave unto one another only, and thus become "one flesh."[16]

Obviously, such a commandment to these two,

the first husband and wife of the human family, has unlimited implications—social, cultural, and religious as well as physical—but that is exactly my point. As all couples come to that moment of bonding in mortality, it is to be just such a complete union. That commandment cannot be fulfilled, and that symbolism of "one flesh" cannot be preserved, if we hastily, guiltily, and surreptitiously share intimacy in a darkened corner of a darkened hour, then just as hastily, guiltily, and surreptitiously retreat to our separate worlds—not to eat or live or cry or laugh together, not to do the laundry and the dishes and the homework, not to manage a budget and pay the bills and tend the children and plan together for the future. No, we cannot do that until we are truly one—united, bound, linked, tied, welded, sealed, married.

Can you see then the moral duplicity that comes from pretending we are one, sharing the physical symbols and physical intimacy of our union, but then fleeing, retreating, severing all such other aspects—

and symbols—of what was meant to be a total obligation, only to unite again furtively some other night or, worse yet, furtively unite (and you can tell how cynically I use that word) with some other partner who is no more bound to us, no more one with us than the last was or than the one that will come next week or next month or next year or anytime before the binding commitments of marriage?

You must wait until you can give everything, and you cannot give everything until you are at least legally and, for Latter-day Saint purposes, eternally pronounced as one. To give illicitly that which is not yours to give (remember, "you are not your own") and to give only part of that which cannot be followed with the gift of your whole heart and your whole life and your whole self is its own form of emotional Russian roulette. If you persist in sharing part without the whole, in pursuing satisfaction devoid of symbolism, in giving parts and pieces and inflamed fragments only, you run the terrible risk of such spiritual, psychic damage that you may undermine both your physical intimacy and your wholehearted devotion to a truer, later love. You may come to that moment of real love, of total union, only to discover to your horror that what you should have saved has been spent and that only God's grace can recover that piecemeal dissipation of your virtue.

A good Latter-day Saint friend, Dr. Victor L. Brown Jr., has written of this issue:

"Fragmentation enables its users to counterfeit intimacy. . . . If we relate to each other in fragments, at best we miss full relationships. At worst, we manipulate and exploit others for our gratification. Sexual fragmentation can be particularly harmful because it gives powerful physiological rewards which, though illusory, can temporarily persuade us to overlook the serious deficits in the overall relationship. Two people may marry for physical gratification and then discover that the illusion of union collapses under the weight of intellectual, social, and spiritual incompatibilities. . . .

"Sexual fragmentation is particularly harmful

because it is particularly deceptive. The intense human intimacy that should be enjoyed in and symbolized by sexual union is counterfeited by sensual episodes which suggest—but cannot deliver—acceptance, understanding, and love. Such encounters mistake the end for the means as lonely, desperate people seek a common denominator which will permit the easiest, quickest gratification."[17]

Listen to a far more biting observation by a non-Latter-day Saint regarding such acts devoid of both the soul and the symbolism we have been discussing. He writes: "Our sexuality has been animalized, stripped of the intricacy of feeling with which human beings have endowed it, leaving us to contemplate only the act, and to fear our impotence in it. It is this animalization from which the sexual manuals cannot escape, even when they try to do so, because they are reflections of it. They might [as well] be textbooks for veterinarians."[18]

In this matter of counterfeit intimacy and deceptive gratification, I express particular caution to the men who read this message. I have heard all my life that it is the young woman who has to assume the responsibility for controlling the limits of intimacy in courtship because a young man cannot. Seldom have I heard any point made about this subject that makes me more disappointed than that. What kind of man is he, what priesthood or power or strength or self-control does this man have, that lets him develop in society, grow to the age of mature accountability, perhaps even pursue a university education and prepare to affect the future of colleagues and kingdoms and the course of the world, yet he does not have the mental capacity or the moral will to say, "I will not do that thing"? No, this sorry drugstore psychology would have us say, "I just can't help myself. My glands have complete control over my life—my mind, my will, my entire future."

To say that a young woman in such a relationship has to bear her responsibility and that of the young man too is one of the most inappropriate suggestions I can imagine. In most instances if there is sexual transgression, I lay the burden squarely on the shoulders of the young man—for our purposes probably a priesthood bearer—and that's where I believe God intended responsibility to be. In saying that, I do not excuse young women who exercise no restraint and have not the character or conviction to demand intimacy only in its rightful role. Unfortunately, I have had enough experience in Church callings to know that women as well as men can be predatory, a phenomenon more and more evident (and more and more tragic) in modern times. But I also refuse to accept the feigned innocence of some young man who wants to sin and calls it psychology.

Indeed, most tragically, it is the young woman who is most often the victim; it is the young woman who most often suffers the greater pain; it is the young woman who most often feels used and abused and terribly unclean. And for that imposed uncleanliness the man as well as the woman will pay, as surely as the sun sets and rivers run to the sea.

Note the prophet Jacob's straightforward language

on this account in the Book of Mormon. After a bold confrontation on the subject of sexual transgression among the Nephites, he quotes Jehovah: "For behold, I, the Lord, have seen the sorrow, and heard the mourning of the *daughters* of my people in the land. . . . And I will not suffer, saith the Lord of Hosts, that the cries of the fair *daughters* of this people . . . shall come up unto me against the *men* of my people, saith the Lord of Hosts.

"For they shall not lead away captive the *daughters* of my people because of their tenderness, save I shall visit them with a sore curse, even unto destruction."[19]

Don't be deceived and don't be destroyed. Unless such fire is controlled, your clothes and your future will be burned, and your world, short of painful and perfect repentance, can go up in flames. I give that to you on good word: I give it to you on God's word.

# SACRAMENTAL
# MOMENTS

*Sexual union is . . . a sacrament*

*of the highest order, a union not*

*only of a man and a woman but*

*very much the union of that man*

*and that woman with God.*

T*hird, after soul and symbol comes the word sacrament, a term closely related to the other two.*

Sexual intimacy is not only a symbolic union between a man and a woman—the uniting of their very souls—but it is also symbolic of a union between mortals and deity, between otherwise ordinary and fallible humans uniting for a rare and special moment with God Himself and all the powers by which He gives life in this wide universe of ours.

In this latter sense, human intimacy is a kind of sacrament, a very special symbol. For our purpose, a sacrament could be any one of a number of gestures or acts or ordinances that unite us with God and His limitless powers. We are imperfect and mortal; He is perfect and immortal. But from time to time— indeed, as often as is possible and appropriate—we find ways and go to places and create circumstances where we can unite symbolically with Him and, in so doing, gain access to His power. Those special moments of union with God are sacramental moments, such as kneeling at a marriage altar or blessing a newborn baby or partaking of the emblems of the Lord's Supper. This latter ordinance is the one we in the Church have come to associate most traditionally with the word *sacrament,* though it is technically only one of many such moments when we formally take the hand of God and feel His divine power.

These are moments when we quite literally unite our will with God's will, our spirit with His Spirit, where communion through the veil becomes very real. At such moments we not only acknowledge His divinity, but we also quite literally take something of that divinity to ourselves. Such are the holy sacraments.

Now, I know of no one who would rush into a sacramental service, grab the linen from the tables, throw the bread the full length of the room, tip the water trays onto the floor, and laughingly retreat from the building to await an opportunity to do the same thing at another worship service the next Sunday. No one would do that during one of the truly sacred moments of our religious worship. Nor would anyone violate any of the other sacramental moments in our lives, those times when we consciously claim God's power and by invitation stand with Him in privilege and principality.

But I wish to stress, as my third of three reasons to be clean, that sexual union is also, in its own profound way, a sacrament of the highest order, a union not only of a man and a woman but very much the union of that man and that woman with God. Indeed, if our definition of sacrament is that act of claiming, sharing, and exercising God's own inestimable power, then I know of virtually no other divine privilege so routinely given to us all—women or men, ordained or unordained, Latter-day Saint or non-Latter-day Saint—than the miraculous and majestic power of transmitting life, the unspeakable, unfathomable, unbroken power of procreation. There are those special moments in our lives when the other, more formal ordinances of the gospel—the sacraments, if you will—allow us to feel the grace and grandeur of God's power. Many are one-time experiences (such as our own confirmation or our own marriage), and some are repeatable (such as administering to the sick or doing ordinance work for others in the temple). But I know of nothing so earth-shatteringly powerful and yet so universally and unstintingly given to us as the God-given power available in every one of us from our early teen years on to create a human body, that wonder of all wonders, a genetically and spiritually unique being never before seen in the history of the world and never to be duplicated again in all the ages of eternity: a child, *our* child—with eyes and ears and fingers and toes and a future of unspeakable grandeur.

Imagine that, if you will. Veritable teenagers—and all of us for many decades thereafter—carrying daily, hourly, minute-to-minute, virtually every waking and sleeping moment of our lives, the power and the chemistry and the eternally transmitted seeds of life to grant someone else her second estate, someone else his next level of development in the divine plan of salvation. I submit to you that no power, priesthood or otherwise, is given by God so universally to so many with virtually no control over its use except *self*-control. And I submit that we will never be more like God at any other time in this life than when we are expressing that particular power. Of all the titles He has chosen for Himself, Father is the one He declares, and creation is His watchword—especially human creation, creation in His image. His glory isn't a mountain, as stunning as mountains are. It isn't in sea or sky or snow or sunrise, as beautiful as they all are. It isn't in art or technology, be that a concerto or computer. No, His glory—and His grief—is in His children. We—you and I—are His prized possessions, and we are the earthly evidence, however inadequate, of what He truly is. Human life is the greatest of God's powers, the most mysterious and magnificent chemistry of it all, and you and I have been given it, but under the most serious and sacred of restrictions. You and I—who can make neither mountain nor moonlight, not one rain-drop or a single rose—have this greater gift in an absolutely unlimited way. And the only control placed on us is self-control—self-control born of respect for the divine sacramental power it is.

Surely God's trust in us to respect this future-forming gift is an awesomely staggering one. We who may not be able to repair a bicycle or assemble an average jigsaw puzzle can yet, in all of our weaknesses and imperfections, carry this procreative power which makes us so very much like God in at least that one grand and majestic way.

# A SERIOUS MATTER

"*Sex is a river of fire that must be banked and cooled by a hundred restraints if it is not to consume [us] in chaos.*"

—*Will and Ariel Durant*

*ouls. Symbols. Sacraments.* Do these words suggest why human intimacy is such a serious matter? Why it is so right and rewarding, so stunningly beautiful when it is within marriage and approved of God (not just "good" but "*very* good"),[20] and so blasphemously wrong—like unto murder—when it is outside such a covenant? It is my understanding that we park and pet and sleep over and sleep with at the peril of our very lives. Our penalty may not come on the precise day of our transgression, but it comes surely and certainly enough, and were it not for a merciful God and the treasured privilege of personal repentance, far too many would even now be feeling that hellish pain which, like the passion we have been discussing, is also always described in the metaphor of fire. Someday, somewhere, sometime the morally unclean will, until they repent, pray like the rich man, wishing Lazarus to "dip . . . his finger in the water, and cool my tongue; for I am tormented in this flame."[21]

In closing, consider this from two students of civilization's long, instructive story:

"No one man [or woman], however brilliant or well-informed, can come in one lifetime to such fullness of understanding as to safely judge and dismiss the customs or institutions of his society, for these are the wisdom of generations after centuries of experiment in the laboratory of history. A youth boiling with hormones will wonder why he should not give full freedom to his sexual desires; and if he is unchecked by custom, morals, or laws, he may ruin his life [or hers] before he matures sufficiently to understand that sex is a river of fire that must be banked and cooled by a hundred restraints if it is not to consume in chaos both the individual and the group."[22]

Or, in the more ecclesiastical words of Elder James E. Talmage:

"It has been declared in the solemn word of revelation, that the spirit and the body constitute the soul of man; and, therefore, we should look upon this body as something that shall endure in the resurrected state, beyond the grave, something to be kept pure and holy. Be not afraid of soiling its hands; be not afraid of scars that may come to it if won in earnest effort, or [won] in honest fight, but beware of scars that disfigure, that have come to you in places where you ought not have gone, that have befallen you in unworthy undertakings [pursued where you ought not have been]; beware of the wounds of battles in which you have been fighting on the wrong side."[23]

If some are feeling the "scars . . . that have come to you in places where you ought not have gone," to them is extended the special peace and promise available through the atoning sacrifice of the Lord Jesus Christ. His love and the restored gospel principles and ordinances that make His love available to us with all their cleansing and healing power are freely given. The power of these principles and ordinances, including complete and redeeming repentance, are fully realized only in this, the true and living Church of the true and living God. We should all "come unto Christ"[24] and be morally clean in order to claim all the blessings of love—His love for us, our love for Him, and a couple's truest love for each other.

## Notes

1. *The Decline and Fall of the Roman Empire*, vol. 40 of *Great Books of the Western World*, 1952, 92.

2. In *New Hampshire* (New York: Henry Holt, 1923), 80.

3. Proverbs 6:27–28, 32–33.

4. Alma 39:5; emphasis added.

5. Proverbs 30:20.

6. Proverbs 6:32.

7. D&C 88:15; emphasis added.

8. D&C 93:34.

9. See Matthew 8:28–32.

10. Conference Report, October 1913, 117.

11. "The Very Key," filmstrip based on a talk by Elder Boyd K. Packer (Salt Lake City: The Church of Jesus Christ of Latter-day Saints, 1987).

12. Hebrews 6:6.

13. 1 Corinthians 6:13–20; emphasis added.

14. See D&C 132:19, 24.

15. See D&C 128:18.

16. Genesis 2:24.

17. *Human Intimacy: Illusion & Reality* (Salt Lake City: Parliament Publishers, 1981), 5–6.

18. Fairlie, *The Seven Deadly Sins Today* (Notre Dame, Ind.: University of Notre Dame Press, 1979), 182.

19. Jacob 2:31–34; emphasis added.

20. Genesis 1:31.

21. Luke 16:24.

22. Will and Ariel Durant, *The Lessons of History* (New York: Simon & Schuster, 1968), 35–36.

23. Conference Report, October 1913, 117.

24. Moroni 10:30, 32.

## *About the Author*

Elder Jeffrey R. Holland was called as a member of the Quorum of the Twelve Apostles of The Church of Jesus Christ of Latter-day Saints in June 1994. A native of St. George, Utah, he has spent most of his professional life in Church education. He received a bachelor's and master's degree from Brigham Young University, and a master's degree and Ph.D. from Yale University.

In 1974 he became Dean of Religious Instruction at BYU. Two years later, he was named Church Commissioner of Education. In 1980 he was appointed president of BYU, the position in which he was serving when sustained as a member of the First Quorum of the Seventy in 1989.

Elder Holland and his wife, Patricia Terry Holland, are the parents of three children.

SKU 4057551 U.S. $12.95

SKU 4057551 U.S. $12.95

UPC

6 45857 83027 7

EAN

9 781573 458597

51295

ISBN 1-57345-859-7